KRUGER

NATIONAL PARK

DAVID ROGERS

STRUIK

CONTENTS

GET-OUT POINTS AND PICNIC SITES

Afsaal is a large picnic site and has toilets, shade, seating, braai areas, boiling water, cooking gas, a shop and hot refreshments.

Albasini Ruins has an educational display.

Babalala has toilets, shade, seating, braai areas, boiling water, cooking gas and cool drinks. A major attraction is an enormous fig tree which harbours a wealth of birdlife, including green pigeons, wattled starlings and plumcoloured starlings.

Crocodile Bridge Gate has toilets, shade, seating, braai areas, boiling water, cooking gas, a shop and a telephone.

Crocodile River's hippo pool has no facilities. A guide will accompany you to view the hippo pool and crocodiles. This is a good spot for water birds, including water dikkops, whitefaced duck and the rare African finfoot.

Kruger Tablets has no facilities.

Masorini has toilets, shade, seating, braai areas, boiling water, cooking gas, cool drinks and an educational display (Iron-Age village, smelting works and guided walks).

Mlondozi Dam has toilets, shade, seating, braai areas, boiling water, cooking gas and cool drinks.

Mooiplaas has toilets, shade, seating, braai areas, boiling water, cooking gas and drinks.

Muzandzeni has toilets, shade, seating, braai areas, boiling water, cooking gas and cool drinks.

Nhlanguleni has toilets, shade, seating, braai areas, boiling water, cooking gas and cool drinks.

Nkhulu has toilets, shade, seating, braai areas, boiling water, cooking gas, a shop, hot refreshments and cool drinks.

Nwanetsi has toilets, shade, seating, braai areas, boiling water, cooking gas, cool drinks and an educational display, and Sweni bird hide south of Nwanetsi.

Orpen Dam has toilets, shade and seating.

Pafuri has toilets, shade, seating, braai areas and boiling water.

Rabelais Museum has an educational display.

Shingwedzi's bird hide at Kanniedood Dam has an educational display.

Skukuza has an indigenous plant nursery.

Stevenson-Hamilton's Memorial has no facilities.

Timbavati has toilets, shade, seating, braai areas, boiling water, cooking gas and cool drinks.

Tshanga has toilets and shade.

Tshokwane has toilets, shade, seating, braai areas, boiling water, cooking gas, shop, hot refreshments and cool drinks.

Tulamela has Iron-Age stone ruins.

Unravelling the Clues of Vegetation

A visitor's wilderness experience will be greatly enhanced by an understanding of the habitats frequented by the various animal species. The park encompasses more than thirty different botanical areas, with the vegetation of each influenced by a wide variety of soil types and topographical features. Four of these areas are major zones, an understanding of which may assist you in planning your route.

The Olifants River, which cuts across the centre of the park, acts as boundary between three major areas. The largest of these extends north to the Luvuvhu River and is dominated by vast plains of mopane trees and red-bush willow punctuated by bulky baobabs. This is the home of some of the largest elephant herds in the national park as well as less common species such as sable, eland, tsessebe and ostrich.

South of the Olifants River and extending eastward to the foothills of the Lebombo Mountains is the park's second-largest botanical area, dominated by some of the sweetest grazing in the park. In this region large concentrations of wildlife, including zebra, impala, wildebeest and buffalo, are encountered.

Wherever these animals are found in great herds, you can be assured that a host of predators are nearby.

West of this area lies the wettest and most mountainous region of the park, where one finds an astounding array of thick stands of trees and bushes. Large numbers of rhino, kudu and leopard occur here. The grassland is less sweet here than in other areas, so generally fewer grazers are seen, though seasonal migrations may bring more of them to this region.

The smallest and perhaps the most interesting areas are the densely vegetated riverine communities which occur throughout the park. Here one finds the greatest variety of vegetation, including fever, leadwood and sycamore fig trees. A visitor who stays close to the rivers is assured of seeing a wide variety of wildlife. One particularly notable riverine community is the tropical forest area near Pafuri in the northern reaches of the park. Huge wild fig and sausage trees (with their large sausage-shaped seed pods) as well as Natal mahogany, blackthorn and Transvaal mustard trees are common. Birds include African fish eagles, kingfishers and herons.

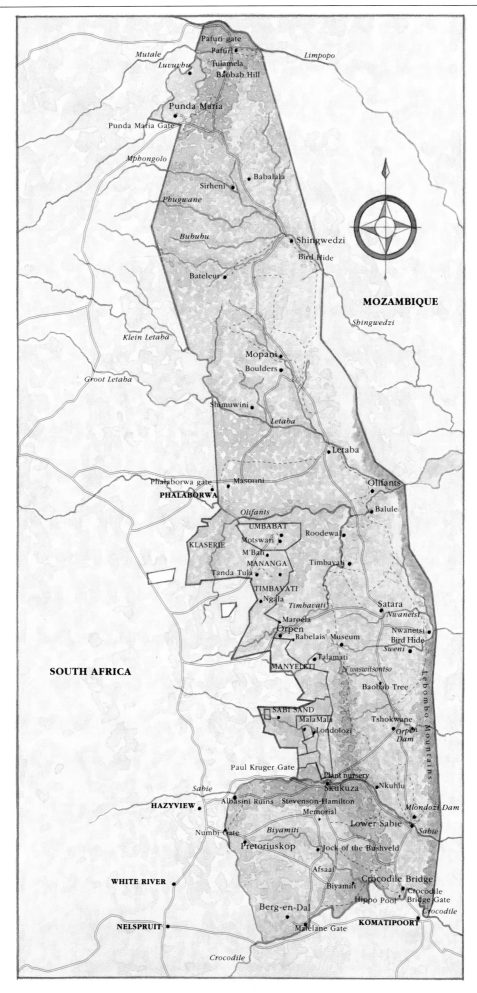

KRUGER NATIONAL PARK

The people's wilderness

On a vast expanse of African soil conservationists have created an almost pristine wilderness where a unique wildlife experience awaits visitors. It is an enormous accomplishment – one which ensures that for many generations to come there is a place close to nature where one can renew the spirit.

It has taken a century to bring the Kruger National Park to its present pinnacle of conservation excellence. Today it is one of the ten largest wildlife reserves in the world, and therefore justly earns its status as one of the great game parks of Africa as well.

A pocket of nature which allows you to see elephant, lion, rhinoceros, buffalo and leopard – the famous Big Five – as well as giraffe and huge herds of antelope, wildebeest, hippopotamus and much more besides, as freely as one can in the Kruger National Park, must be rich indeed. In fact the park is densely populated by about 520 bird, 34 amphibian, 116 reptile and 148 mammal species, each of which occupies a particular niche within a broad range of habitats, ranging from arid grasslands to lush subtropical woodlands.

The present Kruger National Park is immense, covering 19 685 square kilometres – an area almost the size of Wales or two thirds of Belgium. It is bordered by the Lebombo Mountains to the east and the Escarpment to the west and extends about 350 kilometres north-south along the border between South Africa and Mozambique in an area known as the Mpumalanga Lowveld.

There are more than 3 000 kilometres of excellent roads from which one can explore the park. The camps have modern facilities, including air conditioning, to ensure that a visitor's intimate African experience is also a comfortable one.

The park's game drives – the best of which are described in the main section of this book – are regarded by many as the most rewarding in Africa, offering visitors the opportunity to enjoy close encounters with a huge variety of wildlife.

OPPOSITE: *It looks like a telling of tales, but there's no secret about the relationship between impala and redbilled oxpecker.*
It's a mutually beneficial one, as the oxpecker delicately removes and feeds on parasitic insects that infest the impala's hide and the more tender skin inside the ears.
ABOVE: *Although the yellowthroated longclaw makes its bulky nest of grass or reeds on the ground, it often perches on trees to call or to hawk insects.*

During the past few centuries humans have become one of the most numerous – and most destructive – species ever to inhabit this planet. Ironically, humans are now also the only hope for its survival. One of the great success stories in this regard gradually unfolded during the past century as conservationists did their utmost to ensure that generations to come will have much the same view of the Mpumalanga Lowveld as was enjoyed some half a million years ago by its earliest Stone Age hunter-gatherer inhabitants. Descendants of these earliest inhabitants, namely the San (Bushmen), have left fascinating glimpses of their world throughout the park in the form of more than 100 intriguing rock art sites which depict hunting scenes and their living conditions.

In addition to such evidence of very early communities, over 300 Iron Age sites dating back 1 500 years have been identified in the Kruger National Park by the Archaeology Department of the University of Pretoria. In fact, iron smelting was still being practised for a living by the local baPhalaborwa tribe as late as the last century, to a large degree because tsetse flies often infected cattle with the deadly *nagana* disease, which made stock-farming unviable. Until the arrival of Europeans, these craftsmen (whose lifestyle is depicted at the Masorini historical site – see p 36) dominated the area, having succeeded in forcing other inhabitants such as the San west towards the arid Kalahari.

During the 18th century, however, Europeans driven by a desire for adventure and wealth (hides, skins, ivory and rumours of gold) began to infiltrate the Lowveld and brought with them the potential for environmental disaster.

The first of these explorers was François de Cuiper, who in 1725 led a Dutch East India Company expedition into the region from Delagoa Bay (present-day Maputo). The expedition was attacked by local inhabitants near Gomondwane, however, and beat a hasty retreat. In 1836 Voortrekker expeditions under Hans van Rensburg and Louis Trichardt travelled through the area to Delagoa Bay but met with hardship and tragedy, enhancing the Lowveld's reputation as a dangerous and unhealthy place. Only from 1845 onwards was a more permanent European presence established when a Portuguese trader named João Albasini set up a string of trading posts in the area, including one north of present-day Pretoriuskop.

Soon after, the burghers of the Zuid-Afrikaansche Republiek (ZAR – Transvaal Republic), realising that Delagoa Bay was their closest access to the sea, established a wagon trail from Ohrigstad to the Portuguese port of Lourenço Marques. Early traders and transport riders (such as Sir Percy Fitzpatrick – see p 10) travelling

RIGHT: *The symbiotic relationship of giraffe and redbilled oxpecker. The critical interdependence of animals, birds and plants, misunderstood in the park's early days, is now keenly appreciated by conservationists.*
OPPOSITE TOP: *James Stevenson-Hamilton, father of the Kruger National Park, was one of the country's earliest conservationists.*
OPPOSITE RIGHT: *Towards the early part of the century elephant numbers in the region dwindled to fewer than 100 animals.*

through the Lowveld braved many dangers, including predators and the equally deadly, albeit less conspicuous, tsetse fly and mosquito. These pioneers made regular trips between Lourenço Marques and present-day Mpumalanga, bringing much-needed provisions to towns, farms and mining camps in the area, but their role was first diminished and then made redundant by the completion of a railway line between Pretoria and Lourenço Marques in 1894.

Malaria, sleeping sickness, *nagana* and African horse sickness made the Lowveld unsuitable for farming, but it was a hunter's paradise, to such an extent that many

species were soon in grave danger of vanishing for ever. Fortunately the trend was countered, before it was too late, by the efforts of a few dedicated individuals, and none more so than Paul Kruger – president of the ZAR.

Kruger's was the first voice raised in alarm at the demise of the once great animal herds of Mpumalanga to be taken seriously. Less interested, perhaps, in conservation for its own sake than in ensuring adequate stock for future hunting, Kruger nevertheless argued before his Cabinet in 1889 that 'continued shooting by farmers, poachers and others would destroy a valuable national asset'. Kruger's colleagues were shocked that he should propose depriving people of what they regarded as their natural right to hunt where and when they pleased, but he persevered, and nine years later his efforts were crowned with success when an area of approximately 4 600 square kilometres between the Crocodile and Sabie rivers was proclaimed as the Sabie Game Reserve.

The intervention of the Boer War (1899 – 1902) and the occupation of the then Transvaal by British forces could have spelled the end of Kruger's vision, but in 1902 James Stevenson-Hamilton was appointed Sabie's head ranger with the instruction to

make himself 'thoroughly disagreeable' to poachers – white and black – who used various traps and snares to kill animals not only for their meat, but their hides and horns as well. So strict was he in carrying out his duties, for example by prevailing on Mozambican tribes to move back across the border, that the locals soon named him Skukuza – 'he who sweeps clean'.

A year later an area north of the Letaba River that had been newly proclaimed as the Shingwedzi Game Reserve was also placed under his control.

The area under Stevenson-Hamilton's control continued to expand and by 1905 his staff of five rangers and several game scouts were required to keep free from poachers and hunters an area of some 17 000 square kilometres. Many of these bandits operated from the north-eastern corner of the reserve at 'Crooks' Corner'. This was the junction of the borders of South Africa, Southern Rhodesia (Zimbabwe) and Mozambique and notorious ivory hunters took refuge here in the knowledge that they could slip across the border into one of the countries to escape the authorities in another.

Stevenson-Hamilton also had great trouble in countering the efforts of those who sought to exploit economic opportunities in

A Transport Rider and his Dog

In the southern areas of the Kruger National Park you will notice plaques commemorating a famous dog named Jock, who became a Lowveld legend following the publication of the epic story *Jock of the Bushveld*. Written by Sir Percy FitzPatrick in 1907, the book has never been out of print and has sold millions of copies worldwide.

FitzPatrick was a transport rider during the 1890s and the book is an autobiographical account of this period in his life, which was shared by his dog Jock. Their journeys between Lourenço Marques and the gold fields of Barberton and Lydenburg were filled with adventure as they faced predators, tsetse fly and malaria-carrying mosquito.

In 1889 FitzPatrick's six years as a transport rider ended abruptly when tsetse fly infected all of his cattle with deadly *nagana*. He returned to Barberton to find secure employment and married a woman named Lilian Cubitt. Sadly, Jock could not adapt to town life and with great reluctance FitzPatrick had to give his faithful companion away to a more suitable home.

One night a stray dog attacked chickens on the farm where Jock lived. Showing his true hunting-dog spirit, Jock killed the chicken-thief but sadly his master, who had also been woken, mistook Jock for the stray and fired a shot which killed him instantly.

Percy FitzPatrick – at that stage a highly successful businessman and politician who had been knighted in 1902 – wrote his book after being encouraged to do so by his children and the renowned author Rudyard Kipling.

The first edition of *Jock of the Bushveld* is particularly valuable. It also contains a curious flaw. Illustrator Edmund Caldwell, who travelled to present-day Mpumalanga to do research for the book, clearly was not as intimate with the bush as the author, or he would have known that dung beetles roll droppings backwards, not forwards, as his illustration reveals.

the Lowveld. Mining prospectors were active in an area separating the two game reserves; a railway line running through the reserve to Selati was completed in 1912; and farmers – some of them within a few kilometres of the reserve – complained that disease-carrying game and predators were killing their livestock. Reluctantly, Stevenson-Hamilton and his men were forced to cull lion in border areas and to accommodate sheep-farmers who had winter grazing rights within the reserve.

A reason other than simply conserving game for its own sake was needed to justify the reserve's continued existence. In the mid-1920s Stevenson-Hamilton was made aware that the reserve had tourist potential, and he set about exploiting it. When he heard that the South African Railways was planning a nine-day tour of the Lowveld by train, he arranged for an overnight stop at Sabie Bridge to be included in the itinerary. Much to everybody's surprise, the sights and sounds of the bushveld proved the highlight of the tour.

As public knowledge of the park grew, so did support for its continued preservation. On 31 May 1926 the Sabie and Shingwedzi game reserves and the 70 privately owned farms separating them were

consolidated into the Kruger National Park. A key provision of the Act of Parliament by which the park was established, was that it should be preserved in its natural state not only for posterity but also for the enjoyment of visitors.

To Stevenson-Hamilton and his team, the visitors' enjoyment of the park brought new challenges and a considerable amount of hard work as they found themselves becoming more and more involved in the accommodation business. Early visitors to the park had to camp in the open and found that there were very few roads, but by the end of 1936 approximately 1 400 kilometres of roads and hundreds of

rondavels had been constructed to cater for an annual influx of some 26 000 people.

On his retirement in 1946, Stevenson-Hamilton, undeniably 'the father of the Kruger National Park', reflected on his past 44 years: 'I had at least brought up Cinderella and launched her on her career. I loved her best when she was a pathetic and dust-covered little wench, derided and abused. Always I felt that, given her chance, and her attractions recognised, unlimited possibilities lay before her. Now that she had become a Great Lady it was fitting she should be provided with custodians perhaps better suited to provide her new requirements.'

OPPOSITE: *Slow and careful drivers – and their passengers – learn to look for spoor in the thicker dust by the sides of the park's many kilometres of gravel roads.*
LEFT: *When zebra fight, they make free use of tooth and hoof, but this encounter would appear to be a small misunderstanding rather than a serious contest.*
BELOW: *Lions' lovemaking can be intense. During oestrus, copulation may occur almost every twenty minutes.*

CONSERVATION - *Cinderella Enters the Scientific Age*

In the period following World War II the tenacity and love for nature displayed by Stevenson-Hamilton made way for the ideas of a new generation of wardens. Research and science replaced the horse and rifle as the tools they used to face up to different environmental and economic challenges.

The establishment of a research station at Skukuza in 1950 heralded the start of this new era, and nine years later construction began on a 1 800-kilometre fence around the perimeter of the park. While lion and elephant would no longer have to be shot if they roamed into neighbouring land, and disease was less likely to spread from buffalo to livestock, the fence cut off traditional migration routes and created new problems which would need careful management.

Today, the Kruger National Park has a highly skilled team of almost 4 000 people who monitor and control water resources, fire, vegetation, migration, population and disease. Without their intervention the balance between the needs of tourism and of nature could not be maintained and the structure of the park would collapse.

An aim of the park is to maximize biodiversity and to conserve all sensitive habitats and species. Not only is this essential for the preservation of these species, but it also ensures some of the most rewarding game viewing in the world. Careful management of water and fire has resulted in populations of some 100 000 impala, 31 000 zebra, 21 000 buffalo and 14 000 wildebeest.

Were nature to be left to its own devices, this hemmed-in area with its limited water supply (river levels are generally lower now than during the early part of the century) would not be able to sustain the full complement of species. When rivers dry up during winter, the water supply is therefore maintained by the 280 boreholes and 63 dams which have been constructed throughout the park. Yet, despite these supplies, animal numbers can decrease by as much as 30 per cent during times of drought as a result of a lack of grazing.

These artificial water supplies have an added benefit in that they attract herds away from limited and isolated drinking places, which otherwise would be irreparably damaged by overgrazing. In the natural course of events, the regrowth of grassland is encouraged by fire which is usually sparked off by lightning. The new fire policy in the Kruger Park allows lightning-induced fires to burn over much larger areas than in the past. This causes a more natural mosaic of burnt and unburnt veld which enhances biodiversity. The fact that the Kruger Park is fenced does have a negative effect as well in that animal populations (particularly those with few natural enemies) can become too large. Elephant are a case in point. During the first fifty years of this century the elephant population in the park rose considerably; dwindling herds of fewer than 100 individuals became huge extended families of 1 000 or more. In the post-war period this increase has, in fact, become an elephant population explosion.

By 1967 elephant numbered 6 585, and a year later 1 000 more had been born. With a life span of up to 60 years and destructive feeding habits which include flattening trees at whim, they presented conservationists with a dilemma. Could their numbers be allowed to increase to the detriment of the natural habitat of other animals, or should their numbers be controlled? The decision was not easy, but today culling of elephant and occasionally hippo is one of the more unenviable tasks that face conservationists.

There is a moratorium on elephant culling at present while park officials re-examine their elephant management policy. Relocation to other parks is preferred but the market is very limited. Contraception is being looked into but is not yet an option.

Equally controversial is the issue of ivory. Prior to international bans on the ivory trade (aimed at preserving dwindling herds farther north in Africa), this was an important source of income with which to finance the park's many conservation efforts. At the 1997 CITES Convention, the re-opening of limited trade in ivory was approved, as a result of which it is likely that the ivory and hides, obtained through culling in the park, will shortly be able to be sold and used to pay for activities such as translocating endangered species into and out of the park.

Of course the destruction of genetic material is not the best solution for the Kruger National Park. The long-term ideal would be to expand the park to include far less densely populated reserves in the adjacent Zimbabwe and Mozambique. International talks are well advanced to proclaim a park adjoining the Kruger Park in Mozambique in order to create what will be the largest game reserve in the world, but their success hinges on sound diplomatic relations and political stability in the region.

Apart from the problems created by fences, the Kruger National Park faces eco-nomic pressure as well. Mining companies claim that the coal under its soil is of the highest quality, and the debate between conservationists and industrialists will no doubt continue for some time to come. Ultimately a decision will have be made as to whether the exploitation of this resource could be allowed without a fatal impact on the preservation of this wilderness.

Other conservation challenges and threats have their origin outside the park. The Mpumalanga Lowveld is an important eco-nomic region; while factories are monitored to ensure that they do not spew pollutants into rivers, and poor farming practices are discouraged, such activities do lead to poor water quality and silting up of waterways.

The Kruger Park is a conservation leader and lends considerable support to other game reserves and farms which have at their disposal far fewer resources.

OPPOSITE: *Relocated to the Kruger from KwaZulu-Natal, a white or square-lipped rhino and her calf taste the waters at Berg en Dal.*
LEFT: *Noisy and aggresively competitive feed-ers, white-backed vultures are the commonest carrion-eaters of the savannah bushveld.*
BELOW: *In the early years of the park, the Orpen family donated considerable tracts of land, as well as large sums of money, for creating waterholes. Orpen Dam near Tshokwane is an appropriate reminder.*

BIG GAME - *The Mighty Vegetarians*

It is quite astounding that a diet of leaves, grass, bark, fruit and seeds can sustain such a large number of herbivorous mammals, including those mighty vegetarians the hippopotamus, giraffe and elephant.

Elephant are among the most intelligent and beautiful of all mammals and there are few better places to see them than in the Kruger National Park. A thriving population of some 7 500 individuals are found throughout the park, particularly in the flat mopane plains to the north of the Olifants River. In the area around Olifants, Shingwedzi and Letaba camps you are likely to see some of the truly great tuskers which have made this area famous. During the 1980s this was the domain of seven huge bulls – dubbed the Magnificent Seven – with tusks of up to 3 metres long. For many years their whereabouts were kept a secret to protect them from ivory-greedy poachers, but eventually all died, either by the bullet or from old age. A fitting memorial to them has been erected at Letaba camp. Fortunately there is a new generation of great elephants, and recently 14 individuals with tusks in excess of 45 kilograms each were identified in this area. These bulls are up to 60 years old, and consume 200 kilograms of vegetation and 200 litres of water each day to sustain their massive 7 000-kilogram frames.

Buffalo, which occur in breeding herds of up to 1 000 animals, are also found singly – these lone bulls are irritable and potentially very dangerous animals. Herds are generally more docile, but when they are threatened by their two enemies, man and lion, they will often form a formidable outward-facing laager and fiercely defend their young. There used to be some 30 000 buffalo in the park (about 50 per cent of this number died in the drought of 1992) and they are particularly prevalent alongside elephant in the central and northern mopane plains.

Both black and white **rhinoceros** have been viciously slaughtered throughout Africa by poachers who sell their horns to overseas buyers. These horns are much sought after as knife handles in the Middle East, while Far Eastern cultures use the crushed horn for its medicinal properties. Interestingly, the horn differs from those of other animals, being made up of tightly compressed hair instead of having a bone core and sheath. The Kruger National Park is one of the last places in Africa where large numbers of rhino may be seen. White

LEFT: *Despite their thick skin, elephants can suffer from sunburn, so are seldom found far from water – for drinking, spraying in a cooling stream from their trunks or just wallowing in to create a protective mud pack.*
ABOVE: *Cunning and very intelligent, buffalo are also remarkably placid when undisturbed. A wounded buffalo, though, is reckoned one of the most dangerous animals in the world.*

strong reminder of the damage it can do with its two tusk-like canines, which can grow up to 30 centimetres in length. Hippo weigh up to 1 600 kilograms and are most active at night when they leave the dams and rivers of the park to feed on up to 130 kilograms of grass.

The tallest of all mammals is the **giraffe** which can reach a height of 5 metres. This gives them the exclusive ability to feed on the sweet uppermost leaves of many trees. In so doing, they also play an important role in cross-pollinating trees. Unfortunately, the giraffe's massive neck is also a disadvantage. It has only seven vertebrae (the same number as a human), which makes bending down extremely difficult. One of the most curious sights of the park is watching these animals gradually splaying their front legs in order to drink. Partly because this compromising position makes

rhino (distinguished by the wide mouth) now number 2 500 and although there are only 300 black rhino, their numbers are growing, thanks to close monitoring and relocation from other areas. White rhino are most common in the southern and central areas, with the Berg en Dal area offering the best chance of seeing one. Black rhino generally are found in dense thickets and are seldom seen by tourists.

Another herbivore to be treated with respect is the **hippo**, which surprisingly accounts for more human deaths in Africa than any other mammal. Its seemingly docile yawn is often a display of aggression in response to a perceived threat, and is a

them vulnerable to attack and also because blood circulation to the head is impaired, giraffe will seldom drink for longer than 10 seconds at a time before standing upright. The nearly 5 000 giraffe in the Kruger National Park are most commonly seen in the southern and central areas.

Eland – the largest South African antelope – are noble animals which may weigh up to 800 kilograms but are nevertheless surprisingly agile, having been known to clear 2,5 metre-high fences. They are confined to the woodland savannah north of the Olifants River, with a small herd in the area around Ship Mountain near Pretoriuskop. The areas north of Shingwedzi and near Shimuwini camp offer the best chance to see them. Also found in riverine areas throughout the park, including the vicinity of Sabie and Shingwedzi, is the rare **nyala** (cousin of the more common **kudu**). The **sable** antelope, with its dramatic scimitar-shaped horns, is most often seen west of Tshokwane. By far the most common antelope are the **impala** which are found in all habitats and number over 100 000. Furthermore, about 32 000 **zebra** inhabit the park.

OPPOSITE ABOVE: *With a shoulder height of only 1,5 metres and a mass of 1 600 kilograms, hippo enjoy water for its coolness – and for taking the weight off their short legs.*
OPPOSITE BELOW: *Elephant are competent in the water, using the trunk as a snorkel.*
ABOVE: *The early descriptions of giraffe that reached Europe were so confusing that the animal was named 'camelopard' – suggested by its supposedly camel-like appearance and its spots that resembled a leopard's colouring.*
RIGHT: *The shy nyala, found most often in riverine woodlands in the northern region.*

The large cats and dogs of the bushveld are an imposing spectacle, displaying grace and power and instilling fear. They never fail to capture the imagination of visitors to the Kruger National Park. These great hunters occur widely throughout the park, but are concentrated in the central and eastern areas among the great herds of impala, zebra and wildebeest.

Lion are the largest of the park's cats and are most effective hunters. They usually stalk their prey at night, but sometimes it is possible to see them plan a military-style assault upon unsuspecting prey during the day. They operate in formation, shuffling along with their bellies pressed against the ground until they are within striking distance. They then spring and, if successful, break the back of the unfortunate animal with their powerful forelegs before throttling it to death. Hunting is the domain of the female, although the males will often assist once the prey has been brought down. No matter the degree of involvement of the male, however, he is always first in line to feed. Within the social structure of the pride the male is responsible for defending the pride's territory against encroachment from rival males. These areas can be as large as 100 square kilometres and are patrolled at night, accompanied by much roaring and growling.

The Kruger National Park also boasts a white lion strain. These animals were first discovered in the Timbavati Game Reserve, bordering the park, in the 1970s and have subsequently on several occasions been observed near Tshokwane.

You are most likely to see lion near rivers and dams in the shade of large trees, or concealed behind grass. In the Satara area exceptionally large prides of more than 40 individuals sometimes form. Because of the large size of these prides, they may kill up to three times a day.

The majestic, powerfully built **leopard** are elusive cats and therefore much sought after by game-watchers. Your best chance of seeing these animals is to scan dry riverbeds and the boughs of trees in the rocky, thickly vegetated terrain in the southern and central riverine areas carefully, as a rule either very early or late in the day. You will need to drive slowly, however, as their camouflage is excellent. Leopard often use trees to store their prey out of reach of other predators. On one occasion a particularly strong leopard was seen in its leafy larder, guarding a small giraffe! There are about 1 000 leopard in the park.

LEFT: *Leopard are usually nocturnal hunters and capable of impressive athletic feats. Since they are solitary hunters, they tend to be more cautious than lion, as they cannot afford to be injured.*
BELOW: *Survival of the fittest is the rule for young lion; they are allowed to feed at a kill only when the adults have had their share. This one is a strong candidate for survival.*

Cheetah are the sprint athletes of the cat family. Slight and graceful, they are also perfectly built for speed. If you are fortunate enough to see a cheetah in pursuit of its prey, it could be the highlight of your visit. As a cheetah pursues its prey, it holds its head high and still and uses its powerful tail to balance itself through twists and turns at a speed of up to 100 kilometres per hour! They are the fastest of all land animals, but tire fairly quickly. On account of their high-speed hunting technique, the 200 cheetah in Kruger can be fairly easily spotted in their favourite habitat – the open, grassy plains in the southern and central areas of the park. The most frequent sightings have lately been at Lower Sabie, Berg en Dal and Orpen.

There are about 2 000 **hyaena** in the Kruger National Park. Their reputation as cowardly animals is undeserved, as they are extremely powerfully built, with jaws that can crack large bones with ease. Although they are opportunistic scavengers in the main, they are also efficient hunters and frequently kill wildebeest and other medium-sized herbivores singly or in packs. The melancholy nocturnal cry of the hyaena is one of the most characteristic sounds of the African bush. They often make their dens in culverts underneath roads; one well-known den is near Shingwedzi, where the road from the camp joins the main road, and here one can often watch pups suckling and playing.

Wild dogs hunt their prey in large packs. The dogs will fan out and run the prey down, if necessary chasing it over long distances. One of Africa's rarest and most endangered predators, wild dogs were hunted ruthlessly at the turn of the century. Their sociable nature means that they are particularly at risk from diseases such as distemper and rabies, which can spread rapidly and kill a whole pack. Today there are only some 5 000 wild dogs in the whole of the African continent, and of these 380 occur in the Kruger National Park.

Wild dogs can be distinguished by their dog-like appearance and large round ears. They are great wanderers and can appear anywhere in the park (wild dogs from the Kruger National Park have been recorded as far afield as neighbouring Mozambique and Swaziland), but most sightings are reported from the areas around Berg en Dal, Pretoriuskop and Punda Maria.

Another dog-like predator is the black-backed jackal, which can be identified by its fawn-coloured coat and black strip along its back. Although they are most active at night, they are often seen in the early morning, especially in the vicinity of a kill.

OPPOSITE TOP: *An adult wild dog, unlike a lion, will hold back to let its young feed first at a kill. Despite this, and its ruthless efficiency as a hunter, numbers of wild dogs appear to be on the decline.*

OPPOSITE BOTTOM: *By no means the coward of popular belief, the spotted hyaena is an enterprising and efficient hunter.*

ABOVE RIGHT: *Fastest of land mammals, and able to reach – but not maintain – speeds of up to 100 kilometres per hour, the cheetah is the most even-tempered and easily domesticated of the big cats.*

RIGHT: *Solitary and nocturnal, civet were once ruthlessly hunted for an anal secretion that is greatly in demand in the perfume trade. Fortunately, a synthetic substitute has been developed.*

BIRDS - *A Twitcher's Paradise*

The Kruger National Park provides endless joy to thousands of enthusiastic bird-watchers each year. It is, after all, home to about 530 species – more than half the total number found in South Africa! An added incentive is that the southernmost limit of many tropical species occurs within the boundaries of the park.

The Pafuri area is the most rewarding in the park. Here you will find crested guineafowl, tropical boubous, Cape parrots and the curious Pel's fishing owl, as well as a host of water birds and raptors. The areas around Shingwedzi, Lower Sabie, Letaba and the dams near Bateleur are excellent for water birds. The haunting call of African fish eagles can be heard resounding through the dam and river areas.

Summer is the best time for bird-watching in the Kruger National Park, as most of the 280 migratory birds found in the park arrive during the hot, wet period in order to breed. A further advantage is that during November and December the camps open their gates at 04h30, which means that one can view nocturnal species such as owls, nightjars and dikkops.

The big game country around Satara offers the best opportunity to see the five vulture species in the park. Hooded and whitebacked vultures are often the first to reach the site of a kill and are followed by whiteheaded, lappetfaced (which is the largest species and dominates the others) and rare Cape vultures. Hooded vultures are most often seen in the central area.

The south-western area of the park has the highest rainfall and the mountains in the Pretoriuskop area boasts many bird species not found elsewhere in the Lowveld, for example yellowfronted tinker barbets and black sunbirds. Skukuza is an excellent place to see sunbirds, purplecrested louries and weavers.

To enjoy the fantastic feathered show in the Kruger National Park, you would do well to explore the camp in which you are staying; many of them offer trails laid out through the indigenous vegetation. Birds are used to human activity, and in some camps it is quite possible to see more than 80 species in a single day. When venturing out in your vehicle, concentrate on the riverine areas, dams and picnic sites which

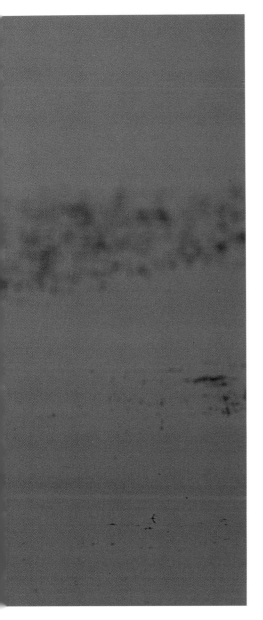

are all well frequented by birds. The dams and rivers to the east are on less porous and more fertile basaltic soils and generally retain water well, thus attracting many water birds. Dams and rivers with exposed mud flats are particularly attractive to water birds such as African jacanas. There are some very rewarding bird hides situated throughout the park, with those at Shingwedzi and Nwanetsi prominent.

While driving through the park, keep a look-out for raptors perched in trees or soaring in thermal currents. Fifteen of the 17 eagle species in South Africa occur in the park. Martial and African fish eagles and bateleurs are exciting species to spot.

Most ornithologists agree that one experiences the best bird-watching by going on one of the wilderness trails through the park, accompanied by a ranger with an intimate knowledge of the bush.

OPPOSITE: *Sometimes confused with herons and cranes, storks – like this yellowbilled stork – have longer bills than cranes, as well as more sturdy bodies and legs than herons.*
TOP: *Usually a ground-feeder, the Cape glossy starling makes the best of a large variety of habitats, from the Namib to KwaZulu-Natal, and can be heard warbling from tree-perches throughout the park.*
ABOVE LEFT: *Fairly common in bush country, the grey hornbill is chiefly a fruit-eater, but will also take insects and small reptiles*
ABOVE RIGHT: *To these redbilled oxpeckers, this impala ram is more than just a casual perch. Its hide provides an important part of their diet of ticks and other insects, as well as hair to use as nesting material.*
RIGHT: *The grey lourie is by no means as glamorous as its Knysna cousin, but has the endearing habit of sometimes helping to feed the chicks of others of its own kind.*

TREES - *The Infinite Variety of the Bushveld*

The Kruger National Park is home to a fascinating range of in excess of 2 000 plants displaying a countless variety of colours, shapes and sizes. These provide a constant source of amazement to anyone with an appreciation of such bounty. On driving through the park you will be travelling through some of the most plant-rich areas in the world. In fact, international botanists regard the Luvuvhu River valley in the extreme north as comparable to the fynbos of the Western Cape as regards its variety of vegetation.

One of the most unusual trees of all is the ancient baobab. Its misshapen, massive trunk topped with a comparatively thin and spindly network of branches evokes great mystery and has inspired many legends, one of which concerns its creation. According to the ancients the baobab once inspired the wrath of God, who was so furious that He threw the tree out of heaven; it fell to earth upside down, with its branches underground and its roots pointing at the sky. Venerable baobabs reach 2 000 years of age and soar to heights of 20 metres, with bulky trunks measuring up to 10 metres across. One of the best examples in the Kruger National Park is found at Baobab Hill near Pafuri, while there are some fine examples inside Mopani camp, which affords visitors a close look.

A popular tree for animals and humans alike is the marula. During summer it has spectacular and highly nutritious foliage and produces a hard round fruit used by many people to make marula beer and jam. The fruit is also a favourite of elephant, kudu and baboon. Growing up to 15 metres, this fairly common deciduous tree can be identified by its distinctive bark which flakes, revealing yellow-pink blotches.

Perhaps the most striking tree of all, and one which is often used by artists as a symbol of the African bushveld, is the umbrella thorn tree. This acacia is unmistakable, standing about 10 metres high, with branches and foliage that extend far out in a symmetrical, umbrella-shaped canopy. It is found throughout the park, but mainly in the Timbavati, Luvuvhu and Tsende areas.

In the northern Luvuvhu areas near Pafuri there are striking groves of trees with distinctive yellow-green trunks. These are fever trees, so named because the early pioneers who camped under them often contracted malaria; in their ignorance they shared the widely-held belief that their fever sprang from the tree instead of from the real culprits – the mosquitoes – which share the same riverside habitat as the tree.

Another magnificent tree which occurs in the riverine forests is the sycamore fig.

These huge trees have a slightly yellowish bark and an extremely distinctive trunk which becomes thick and convoluted near the ground.

The most common tree in the north of the park is the mopane, which covers most of the northern areas as a low and untidy mass of twigs. In a few areas near Punda Maria it does, however, grow into a particularly striking tree up to 18 metres tall. This is a highly nutritious source of food for browsing herbivores, but it also harbours a valuable source of protein fit for human consumption, namely the mopane worm (actually the caterpillar of the mopane emperor moth). The fat caterpillars grow up to 10 centimetres in length and are reasonably tasty when cooked.

Other trees to look for include the jakkalberry, silver terminalia, bush willow and sausage tree with its distinctive sausage-shaped seed pod.

OPPOSITE: *The Olifants River runs west-east and bisects the park roughly in half.*
TOP: *When browsing among the treetops, giraffes use their long tongue, prehensile upper lip and lower incisors to strip away tender leaves.*
ABOVE LEFT: *The vervet monkey is just as at home on the ground or up a tree. Foraging for food keeps them busy for most of the day.*
ABOVE: *During winter this grotesquely proportioned tree is leafless. In South Africa, the baobab is protected by law.*

THE SOUTH

The Hill Country of Kruger

Easy access, a large number of outstanding camps, excellent game drives offering superb opportunities for viewing the area's prolific wildlife, thick vegetation and mountains of granite make the southern stretches the most popular of all in the Kruger National Park.

You can immerse yourself in some of the finest game-viewing areas and historic locations in the south. This is the heart of the original Sabie Game Reserve. An astonishing variety of game may be seen here, particularly in the lower Sabie River region which includes some of the most popular game drives in the park. Historic experiences include a route which follows in the footsteps of the early pioneers and a memorial to the great conservationist James Stevenson-Hamilton.

Berg en Dal

Berg en Dal ('mountain and dale') is nestled in beautiful mountain surroundings in the thickly vegetated south-western region of the Kruger National Park. This is one of the newest and most modern camps in the park and offers visitors outstanding accommodation and facilities.

Everything at Berg en Dal – even the petrol station – has been constructed in such a way that it blends in with the indigenous red bush-willow, marula and acacia vegetation. The huts are designed for maximum privacy and are set in a landscaped garden with large rolling lawns. A highlight of the camp is its large swimming pool with water cascading into it over walls of natural rock. Equally spectacular is the view from the restaurant across the Matjulu Dam. There is excellent bird-watching inside the camp, and nocturnal visitors to the fence line include porcupine, civet and genet.

Visitors who are interested in archaeology will be fascinated by the Iron-Age artifacts which were discovered while the camp was under construction. These may be viewed at the information centre. A 20-minute walk called the Rhino Trail weaves through the camp and includes many items of archaeological, geological and ecological

OPPOSITE: *The Sabie is one of many rivers that flows through the park, but the demands of upstream irrigation seriously reduce the volume available to the wild, and water conservation is of utmost importance.*
ABOVE: *Stepping delicately with its long, splayed toes, the black crake is able to walk across floating vegetation rather like the African jacana.*

interest. A trail with Braille information plates and rope barriers has been designed for blind visitors.

Recommended routes

The environs of Berg en Dal are home to rhino, lion, elephant and cheetah, amongst others, but as the vegetation is fairly thick, the best game routes are towards the more open areas in the vicinity of Crocodile Bridge, Lower Sabie and Skukuza. It is well worth while to drive to nearby Matjulu Hill. On the way to this viewing site one is likely to see many of the specialist trees of the area, including wild olive and seringa. In the evenings the Matjula Dam is a good spot to see wild dog, white rhino and leopard.

Crocodile Bridge

Crocodile Bridge is situated near the entrance to the game-rich eastern areas of the Kruger National Park and is one of the oldest and smallest camps in the park.

Overlooking the Crocodile River, the camp has 20 huts which have been tastefully restored and offer visitors a cosy alternative to some of the larger camps. Guests prepare food in a communal kitchen and can buy basic provisions at the local shop. Visitors should bear in mind that the Crocodile River occasionally bursts its banks during summer and this entrance to the park can then not be used.

Recommended routes
One is permitted to leave one's car at the nearby hippo pool, and it is a rare and exciting experience to hear the grunts and snorts of these large herbivores as they wallow peacefully in the Crocodile River. It is also a good spot for watching water birds, including the African finfoot. There are no facilities here, so it is a good idea to take along a small picnic, but be wary of the resident baboon population, which is likely to try and share your food with you. There is an attendant at the pool who will be happy

to show you a 200-year old San painting which, although it is a little faded and chipped, is a good example of the fine skills of these early residents of the park.

The Gomondwane road to Lower Sabie follows the Vurhami River, and its dams, waterholes and flat terrain provide excellent game-viewing opportunities. The artificially fed waterhole at Gomondwane lies on a wide open plain and is frequented by zebra, wildebeest, impala and cheetah. It is a spectacular view which you will be able to appreciate fully with the use of binoculars. Nearby Gezantombi Dam is frequented by water birds. South of Gomondwane there is a memorial to François de Cuiper, who in 1725 became the first European to venture into the Lowveld. It was here that his expedition was attacked and forced to return to Mozambique. If you make the trip to Gomondwane in the early morning, you will be rewarded with uninterrupted views of the spectacular sunrise over the Lebombo Mountains.

Lower Sabie

Lower Sabie lies in a prime game-viewing region where large herds of antelope – and their attendant predators – congregate to feed from some of the sweetest grazing in the entire park. The camp itself is equally spectacular; nestling in the foothills of the Lebombo Mountains, it provides beautiful views of the procession of animals coming to drink at the Sabie River.

ABOVE LEFT: *A drink means a rare moment of calm in the lives of timid, excitable plains zebras which, when they have satisfied their thirst, will probably break away with a great splash and gallop.*
BELOW LEFT: *In an attractive mountain setting, Berg en Dal is one of the park's larger – and newer – camps.*
ABOVE: *Despite their impressive horns, kudu bulls – like this one feeding on the lush vegetation of early summer – are timid and gentle, and would rather flee than fight.*

It is shady and restful camp dominated by rolling lawns and well-established marula, wild fig, Natal mahogany and fever trees. The diverse vegetation and abundant water of the southern Kruger makes this region outstanding for bird-watching, and you are likely to see purple-crested louries, masked weavers, ducks, herons and kingfishers within the camp.

Accommodation in the camp is charming and many of the huts are grouped together in clusters of three, making this an ideal family camp.

Recommended routes

Game-viewing is generally excellent in this area and on your way to the Mlondozi Dam picnic site you will probably be well rewarded. You may get out of your car at the picnic site and make your way to a thatched shelter from which you may well see elephant, kudu, wildebeest, zebra and cheetah. Bird-watchers will be interested in the abundant bird-life which may include storks and herons. The area towards the Nhlanganzwani Dam to the south of the camp is also worth visiting, and is good for viewing white rhino.

The Lower Sabie road is one of the busiest in the park, with the nickname 'the Piccadilly Highway', so you may choose to avoid it in high season. However, it offers spectacular views of the Sabie River and you may well see a wide variety of game including lion, elephant, buffalo, baboon, leopard and kudu. If you are interested in geology, look out for the unusual outcrop of Clarens sandstone some 20 kilometres outside Lower Sabie camp – it's the same as that occurring in the Free State's Golden Gate Highlands National Park. The Nkuhlu picnic site is a delight, its glorious trees alive with a spectacular array of bird-life. The Salitje road also offers some lovely pools which harbour crocodile, and this is also a good lion area.

Pretoriuskop

Pretoriuskop is 'the friendly camp' and a favourite for many on account of its beautiful trees, prolific bird-life and mountain setting. It is also one of the best maintained, having won the park's best camp trophy on many occasions.

Located in a mountainous region of the park, the camp is set in a beautiful garden graced with marula, Natal mahogany and sycamore trees. There is no better way to stretch your legs after a game drive than to walk among these on the interesting little in-camp trail. However, if you choose, you may also cool off in the attractive rock swimming pool.

Amid the indigenous vegetation you will notice some alien species, such as bougainvillaea. These have been retained for historical reasons as they were planted by the first game warden before the 'indigenous only' rule was established.

Recommended routes

The Fayi loop is the most popular route from Pretoriuskop and takes you through the granite Manungu Hills which offer fine views of the camp and the vast expanse of the Lowveld. There are dense stands of silver terminalia, sicklebush and marula trees and if you are lucky you may see leopard, white rhino, kudu and klipspringer in the area. The route passes a wattle and daub hut which accommodated early tourists to the park in 1930. The Shitlhave Dam lies north-east of Pretoriuskop and is frequented by southern reedbuck and other game.

To the north of Pretoriuskop are the Albisini Ruins – the homestead and trading store of the first European ever to live in the park. João Albasini established a trading station here in 1846 after purchasing the land from Chief Magashula for 22 head of cattle. The site – Magashulaskraal – has been partially reconstructed and one can explore the area on foot and examine artifacts from the period. The area is well shaded by marula and jackalberry trees and is well populated by birds. There is a hippo pool north of the ruins on the Sabie River.

Voortrekker Road takes you past many interesting historical landmarks through an area that is known for wild dog. Ship Mountain was an important landmark to early pioneers, and really does look like an inverted hull! A nearby plaque commemorates the birthplace of the famous dog Jock of the Bushveld (see page 10), while the Outspan plaque marks an area used extensively during the last century as a camping area. The Afsaal picnic site at the junction with the Malelane-Skukuza road is worth a stop, as it is frequented by many birds.

Skukuza

Skukuza, 'the capital of the Kruger National Park', offers visitors a unique experience. As you drive through its impressive gates, you enter a world quite unlike any other in the park. This is the centre of administration and research and is abuzz with scientists, conservationists and game rangers going about their important business.

One of its greatest attractions for visitors is the Stevenson-Hamilton Memorial Library housing a fine collection of ecologically-orientated books, paintings and memorabilia.

OPPOSITE LEFT: *As a family, bee-eaters have long and pointed beaks with a slight curve, short legs and cheerfully bright plumage.*
OPPOSITE RIGHT: *The bateleur is classed by conservationists as 'vulnerable'.*
OPPOSITE BELOW: *Lithe, living scupltures, cheetah were also known as the 'hunting leopard' because, in the Middle East, wealthy people trained them to hunt specific prey.*
BELOW: *Distant hippo taking the waters. Despite being good swimmers, they can also walk confidently along well-travelled paths on the riverbed, completely submerged.*

A wealth of knowledge can be gained in the information centre, while adults and children can attend lectures in the nearby environmental education centre. A museum has been constructed at the railway siding which was used on the Selati line in the 1920s. You can have a meal in a restaurant housed in two old railway carriages from the same period. Also worth a visit is the Campbell 1929 Hut Museum. This National Monument was one of the first tourist

huts to be established at Skukuza and houses interesting relics from the period.

Skukuza has over 200 huts, making it the Kruger's largest camp. In fact, with its hundreds of thousands of visitors each year, it can claim to be one of the largest Lowveld towns. It has an airport, post office, camp doctor, garage and car hire service. Despite this, it is tranquil, with warthog and impala in its gardens.

On the road from Skukuza to Kruger Gate is a turn-off to a plant nursery which specialises in indigenous plants. Here one can buy most of the trees and shrubs seen in the park as well as rare cycads.

Skukuza ('he who sweeps clean') was originally called Sabie Bridge but was renamed in 1936 in honour of James Stevenson-Hamilton, who was given this nickname on account of the effective manner in which he performed his duties. His statue dominates the information centre.

Recommended routes

Skukuza's red bush-willow and acacia vegetation is home to a great variety of game, including lion, elephant and wild dog. The most rewarding routes are those to the east, such as the Lower Sabie road.

South of the camp is De La Porte windmill and also Shirimantanga Hill, where there is a viewpoint and a simple bronze plaque marking the final resting place of James Stevenson-Hamilton and his wife Hilda.

On the northern road to Manzimahle Dam, Nwatindlopfu windmill, Olifants waterhole, Leeupan and Silolweni Dam, one is likely to encounter lion, waterbuck and sable antelope. To reach the Manzimhlope waterhole requires a short detour, but is worth it. During the winter months, it offers an enormous variety of game including large herds of buffalo, wildebeest, zebra and sable (this is the best area for sightings of this species).

A plaque honours Mr J.H. Orpen and his wife Eileen for their donation of seven farms in the western area for incorporation into the Kruger National Park, and another (the Kruger Memorial Tablet) commemorates landmark legislation in 1898 and 1926 which laid the foundation for the proclamation of the Sabie Game Reserve and the Kruger National Park.

Tshokwane is an excellent game-viewing area, known for its albino animals. In addition to white lions, a snow-white kudu bull and a buffalo with white facial markings have been seen. King cheetah – with broad black stripes on their backs – have also been seen in this area, which for some reason seems to produce animals with genetic mutations. When in the area, you may wish to stop at the excellent Tshokwane picnic site, or proceed in order to enjoy the magnificent views from the Nkumbe and Nwamuriwa mountains. You may get out of your car at Nkumbe and nearby Orpen Dam.

OPPOSITE TOP: *Black-backed jackal hunt almost any creature from impala lambs to insects, and will even follow lions in the hope of a place at a feast.*
OPPOSITE LEFT: *Only male waterbuck carry the curved horns, often used to devastating effect in fights over females.*
OPPOSITE RIGHT: *The yellowbilled hornbill is frequently seen throughout the park, usually foraging briskly on the ground.*
ABOVE: *The impala, the most plentiful antelope in the park, number around 100 000.*

CENTRAL KRUGER

The open, grassy plains

The central plains are a popular area for visitors, and this is where you are most likely to see the large predators of the Kruger National Park. The Big Five (lion, elephant, rhino, buffalo and leopard) as well as an outstanding variety of birds are found in this area.

The central region of the Kruger is renowned for its abundant wildlife. The grassy, plains, dotted with acacia and marula trees, are home to a superb variety of herbivores ,attendant predators and many species of birds. Historical sites in the region include recreated village at Masorini.

Letaba

Letaba is favoured by many visitors for its very relaxed atmosphere and indeed presents a welcome sight to weary travellers. It has one of the finest restaurants in the park, with fine views of the procession of animals in the Letaba River valley.

After you have recovered from the long drive, make sure that you explore the information centre. There you will find a display which includes photographs, tusks and information about 'The Magnificent Seven' – a group of huge tuskers which roamed the area in the 1970s and 1980s – and other interesting information on elephant biology.

The spectacular camp boasts noteworthy marula, wild fig and one of the most impressive Natal mahogany trees in the entire park. Furthermore there are stands of tall ilala palms which have been colonised by palm swifts. In fact, bird-watchers should not miss the short in-camp trail, as they will be impressed by the many species present, including mourning doves and brownheaded parrots. Redbilled oxpeckers have been seen at the gate, a group of very tame African fish eagles often perch on the edge of the camp and on the sandbank in front of the restaurant there is a nest of brownthroated martins.

Recommended routes
On the way to Engelhard Dam look out for elephant, klipspringer, lion and the rare Sharpe's grysbok. The dam is one of the largest stretches of water in the park and is

OPPOSITE: *Lion generally hunt in the cool of the afternoon and, on average, make a successful kill in two out of every five attempts.*
ABOVE: *The chief prey of many predators, impala will leap in different directions if attacked in order to confuse their enemy.*

famed for its wealth of bird species. There is always something of interest on the exposed mud flats, for example white-fronted plover, while greyrumped swallows, horus swifts and redwinged pratincoles also occur. Game-watchers should look out for elephant, impala, hippo and crocodile. Nearby, there is an interesting water-ladder which allows fish to swim upstream into the dam from the river below.

The Masorini historical site is well worth a visit. The route takes you past good game-viewing areas including the Nhlanganini Dam, Rhidonda Pan and the windmill at Swartklip.

Mopani

Mopani is the newest camp in the Kruger National Park and also offers some of the most luxurious accommodation. Each of the stone and thatched huts has been carefully designed to blend in with the environment and to offer a high degree of privacy. Although the camp is modern, it has successfully maintained the atmosphere of many far older camps.

The camp has a restaurant, ladies bar, cafeteria and shop as well as a swimming pool, which offers welcome relief, particularly in the hot summer months. An in-camp walk has been laid out to familiarise visitors with the camp's indigenous vegetation, including some fine examples of boaboab trees. It also has facilities for day visitors, including a barbecue area for tour groups and a nursing room for mothers and infants.

The Masorini historical site

One can discover much about the way of life of the Iron-Age inhabitants who lived in this area, long before the establishment of the Kruger National Park, by visiting a fascinating recreated village at Masorini near the Phalaborwa Gate. The museum includes traditional huts and many implements forged and traded by the baPhalaborwa people who lived here as recently as the last century.

Interestingly, archaeological excavations at the site have revealed that Masorini was also used by other Iron- and Stone-Age settlers long before the baPhalaborwa arrived.

Although one can enjoy a great deal of the museum on one's own, there are guided tours of the village, its smelting works and granary. The guide takes visitors up a hill to where the stone-age people lived. It is worthwhile visiting the nearby picnic site.

Recommended routes

In the vicinity of the nearby Pioneer Dam you are likely to see zebra, tsessebe, waterbuck and kudu, and in hot weather this is a very good spot for elephant. Close to Mopani camp is the Mooiplaas picnic site, but for the best game viewing visitors may wish to venture further north or south. Shawu Dam is another good area for elephant, waterbuck and water birds.

Olifants

The panoramic view of the Olifants River and mopane plains to the north of this camp makes a lasting impression on most visitors. The vista one enjoys from the camp restaurant is particularly memorable at sunrise and sunset, particularly as the landscape usually includes elephant and water birds.

Inside the camp an interesting display depicts the ecology of this great river and includes a fresh-water aquarium stocked with indigenous fish. At night, nature films are shown in the open-air amphitheatre.

Bird-watchers will be delighted by the many birds that make their homes in the indigenous trees and flowering shrubs inside the camp's boundaries. Nesting weavers and redwinged starlings are particularly common, and on the banks of the river saddlebilled storks may often be seen. This is also a good place to watch soaring bateleur.

With so much to see and do in and around Olifants, it is not surprising that it has been dubbed 'the lazy man's camp'. If you do decide to venture out, you will notice two spectacular tusks adorning the camp's gates. Although these tusks are artificial, they are so realistic that elephant

have, on occasion, carried them away in order to crush them underfoot in disgust!

Olifants has a small satellite camp called Balule. Park officials once decided to close it, but there was an outcry from traditionalists who had been going there for years. Pressure prevailed and Balule exists as it has for many years with no shops or electricity and a communal kitchen with a paraffin fridge. Balule's huts are reminiscent of the original ones which first housed tourists in the park, with no windows, only a gap between the roof and the walls to permit adequate ventilation.

OPPOSITE: *Long light and shade at Letaba, a medium-sized camp in the central region, and also a junction of three of the national park's major routes.*

TOP: *In its course across the park, the Olifants River is joined by major tributaries the Timbavati and Letaba.*

ABOVE: *Leopard are extremely difficult to spot unless you drive slowly and scrutinise the undergrowth and the overhanging branches of large trees.*

RIGHT: *The giraffe's rudimentary horns, skin-covered, bony extensions of its skull, are used by males when fighting for dominance.*

Recommended routes

The area around Olifants can be thoroughly explored in a morning. There are few roads, yet game-viewing can be very rewarding, particularly along the river-side stretches and from bridges. Bird life in the area includes African jacanas, wattled plovers, goliath herons and, in summer, redbreasted swallows. Elephant abound, as do giraffe, lion and buffalo. If you are lucky you may see nimble klipspringer in rocky areas. West of the camp there is an outstanding view site overlooking the river.

At the Roodewal windmill you may see elephant and giraffe. The Goedgegun waterhole is also rewarding, particularly in the late afternoon. You can get out of your car at Nwamanzi, but there are no facilities.

Orpen

Orpen, the smallest and perhaps the most restful of all camps in the park, is ideal if one is looking for a simpler game reserve experience. Basic provisions are available and guests share a communal kitchen. The camp is named after the Orpen family which generously donated seven farms to the park in the 1930s. Orpen has a satellite camp at Maroela where 20 caravans can be accommodated in a scenic setting near the banks of the Timbavati River. A few kilometres downstream from Maroela is Tamboti, a new tented camp. Accommodation is in furnished safari-style tents.

Recommended routes

The Timbavati River is one of the finest seasonal rivers in the park and the road which follows its course is scenic and provides excellent game-viewing. One of the prime areas along the route is at Leeubron ('lion spring') which is a favourite haunt of these predators. White lion have been spotted here in the past. Kudu, wildebeest, zebra, herons, storks and tame hamerkops can also be seen. In recent years the area has also been good for spotting cheetah.

The picnic site at Timbavati is a haven for a variety of birds which can be enjoyed from the shade of a spreading nyala tree. North of here look out for the large, flat-topped umbrella thorn trees, many of which are surrounded by sharp rocks to discourage elephant from destroying them in their quest for the sought-after seeds.

The Rabelais Museum comprises a hut which houses a small museum display. The nearby dam is frequented by a variety of waterfowl, while the hill at Bobbejaankrans provides excellent views.

Satara

Satara lies in the heart of outstanding game-viewing territory famous for its predators. The tranquil camp is the second largest in the park and has proved particularly popular with overseas visitors. Six large circles of huts are set among great expanses of lawn that are dotted with tall marula, acacia, Natal mahogany and sausage trees.

Satara boasts the most dramatic of all cinemas in the park – an amphitheatre in the open. Its projection room also serves as an information centre which houses numerous interesting exhibits.

The camp was named in interesting circumstances. A 19th-century Indian surveyor was marking out measurements in preparation for settlement by pioneer farmers. As he peered through his theodolite at this site, he jotted down on his map the word 'Satra,' which is Hindi for 17, and from this map the camp was named!

Recommended routes

A good place for photography and game-viewing is to the west at Ngirivani windmill. Although the dam is often dry, visitors can park very close to it on three sides in hope of seeing lion, wild dog, giraffe, buffalo, wildebeest and water birds. Elephant can often be seen here in the middle of the day, playfully cooling off in the water. Nearby Nsemani creek and dam are favourite haunts of African fish eagles and water birds. It is also a good place to spot lion, elephant, impala, waterbuck and hippos.

The area between Satara and the private camp at Nwanetsi is well worth exploring, but to make the most of it, one is recommended to take the gravel S100 road rather than the more direct tarred route. The road hugs the thickly vegetated bank of the Nwanetsi River, but there is open country-side as well, which makes for good game-viewing and photography. According to some visitors their dilemma here has been whether to stay at a leopard kill or proceed further down the road where lion and cheetah have also been successful! For bird-watchers the delight is further on, however, at the Gudzani Dam, where African fish eagles, herons and hamerkops commonly congregate. The Nwanetsi shelter overlooks the Sweni River and here you can admire the wildlife, the birds, the park vistas, the Lebombo Mountains or Chris Eberson's 20 water bird paintings. It is worth while

spending some time exploring the numerous rivers and pools in the area. Just upstream of the Sweni drift is the new Sweni bird hide which offers excellent viewing and photography opportunities.

OPPOSITE LEFT: *Few wild animals associate vehicles with mankind, and these lionesses are unimpressed by the proximity of tourists.*
OPPOSITE RIGHT: *Satara, second-largest camp in the park, is set amid fine grazing land, where large herds and predators may usually be seen.*
TOP: *For a nimble, large-spotted genet, the day's work of finding food begins at nightfall.*
ABOVE: *The African wild cat looks much like its pampered cousin, the domestic cat, with which they readily breed.*
RIGHT: *Nowhere in the park are sable plentiful, a count in 1993 revealing a total of 880 .*

THE NORTH

The remote Kruger National Park

Because they are more remote, the mopane plains of the north are less often frequented by visitors. Those who have travelled through this section will agree however, that it offers some of the most interesting and unspoilt areas to be found anywhere in the park.

Northern Kruger Park is the driest, most remote part but its mopane expanses are roamed by elephant and buffalo, and a huge variety of bird and animal life occur in the pocket of subtropical forest in the northern area at Luvuvhu.

Punda Maria

Punda Maria is situated in one of the most undisturbed areas of the Kruger National Park and the camp is fittingly simple and elegant. The tourist camp was built in the mid-1930s and many of the original huts still stand as a tribute – not only to the builders of those days, but also to the termite-resistant ironwood beams used in their construction. The long white wattle and daub buildings stretch across a well-treed hill slope overlooking vast mopane plains.

The Paradise Flycatcher Trail is so named due to the numbers of these birds to be seen. A further attraction is a family of tame bushbuck. At night a camp attendant spreads out hot red coals in the braai area for anyone wishing to cook meat, a charming tradition usually found only in far smaller

camps. This braai area is often visited by interesting nocturnal species such as genet, porcupine and sometimes civet. Bird species include pennantwinged nightjars, Arnot's chats and yellowbilled oxpeckers.

Punda Maria was established in 1919 as a post from which to monitor ivory poachers Captain J.J. Coetser, the first ranger to be stationed here, gave the camp its curious name. The first species he saw after his arrival was zebra, called punda milia by the Swahili people. Coetser's wife was named Maria, and this seemed a good opportunity to commemorate her, so he named the camp Punda Maria. Although park officials later used the Swahili name, they have since decided that the original name has far more charming connotations.

OPPOSITE: *Despite its impressive bulk, a charging elephant may touch speeds of 40 kilometres per hour, but its ordinary walking pace is around a leisurely 10 kilometres per hour.*
ABOVE: *Unlike others of its kind, the lappet-faced vulture is often a solitary feeder. Apart from its diet of carrion, it may attack small mammals, nestlings, and even fish.*

Recommended routes

The Mahonie loop is a very rewarding round trip of 26 kilometres which takes one through the park's most westerly public roads in an area where lavender, knobbly fig and wild syringa trees thrive on sandveld soils. Maritube Dam is a perfect place to photograph an abundance of bird and animal life, but bear in mind that it dries up in winter. Kudu, nyala and wild dog may be seen in the area around the Witsand and Matukwala dams. A bird hide is planned for the latter to enhance viewing and make it easier for photographers, who are almost assured of good shots in the late afternoon.

The road passes a giant pod mahogany tree ('peulmahonie' in Afrikaans) which gave the drive its name. There is also a magnificent marula tree, protected from elephants by a bed of foot-piercing stones.

Two hills in the area had significance for the former inhabitants. According to legend, Chief Gumbandevu's daughter was a rain-maker. In times of drought farmers would bring her sacrificial animals and gifts. Bearing these offerings, she would go up Gumbandevu Hill to summon rain clouds. At nearby Makahanje Hill is a ruin that was once occupied by a ruler of the same name who, it is said, threw people from this hill into the crocodile-infested waters below as punishment for even the most trivial crimes. Makahanje's deeds soon reached the ears of his half-brother, paramount chief of the area, who had him killed.

The most exciting area in the north is the Luvuvhu River valley; although it involves a long drive, it is well worth a visit.

Of special interest is the Thulamela Iron Age Site (1250–1670) situated south of the Luvuvhu River. The stone structures have been carefully reconstructed and resemble the well-known Zimbabwe Ruins. Potsherds and gold ornaments found here point to the historic trade between the occupants of Thulamela and Arabs. A guide takes visitors up the hill to the stone structures.

Shingwedzi

Shingwedzi has an old-world atmosphere, enhanced by its large grounds and historical buildings. The original buildings have been meticulously restored, but many of the original façades are still intact. In the gardens are ilala palms, cacti, aloes and displays of the famous Shingwedzi impala lily. Bird lovers will notice woodpeckers, glossy starlings, sunbirds and palm swifts.

Luvuvhu, the River of Life

The mighty tree at Baobab Hill was once a landmark to early smugglers and poachers, and a signal that they were near to their hide-out at 'Crooks Corner' where the borders of South Africa, Mozambique and Zimbabwe meet (see page 9). To the modern-day traveller, however, it gives notice that he or she is about to enter one of the most beautiful parts of the Kruger National Park, namely the Luvuvhu River in the Pafuri area.

This oasis of life is quite astounding. Nine major ecosystems meet here and produce a contrasting array of Serengeti-type grasslands, deep valleys, high ridges and deep river gorges. Botanists regard this area as of international importance and second only to the Western Cape as far as the diversity of its plant life is concerned. In the tropical riverine forest there are huge sycamore figs and creepers and this is the playground for troupes of clambering and chattering monkeys. During spring the vegetation is lush, creating a kaleidoscope of colours with bright red flame creepers blooming against stands of ghostly yellow fever trees.

The bird life is equally impressive. Seven bird species with very restricted ranges within the borders of South Africa, including longtailed starlings, yellowbellied sunbirds, Böhm spinetails and mottled spinetails, are found here. At the picnic site at Pafuri you can see various shrike species, narina trogons, African green pigeons and Heuglin's robins. While in the area, you may also see crowned eagles – huge raptors which are quite capable of lifting a small buck!

The hippo in the river, reduced by the drought of 1992-1993 to a mere two, have since increased to 15. There are crocodile, including one of over 5 metres in length, although their numbers have also been reduced. Zebra, buffalo, elephant, nyala and impala may be seen in the area.

Shingwedzi lies in the heart of elephant country and many of the Magnificent Seven, including Mafunyane and Shingwedzi, once roamed the area's flat mopane plains. This is probably the area were one is most likely to encounter large tuskers.

Recommended routes

Kanniedood Dam is a must for lovers of game and birds alike. The riverine ecosystem of the area can be fully appreciated by following the twists and loops of the roads which run along the banks of the dam. A waterside hide gives you the opportunity to observe the dam where dead trees form natural perches for a variety of water birds including darters, kingfishers, herons, storks and ducks. Impala, hippo, buffalo, crocodile, nyala, leopard and elephant are common in the area. There are rewarding drives along the Mphongolo River (good for lion) and south along the gravel road which follows the course of the Shingwedzi River towards Letaba.

OPPOSITE: *The hippo's relatively small, fleshy nostrils automatically close to keep out water as they submerge.*

TOP: *Deceptively languid and clumsy in its proportions, a giraffe in its stride can reach a speed of 56 kilometres per hour, but its principal weapon is its devastating kick.*

LEFT: *The female is the hardest-working member of the lion family. Lionesses do most of the hunting, although the lordly male may consent to administer the coup de grace.*

ABOVE: *A picnic spot near Pafuri in the far north, a region of stunning ecological diversity. It is especially rich in its birdlife.*

THE ALTERNATIVE EXPERIENCE

There is an alternative to staying in the standard accommodation offered at the Kruger National Park, and one which is particularly suited to bird-watchers and those who prefer to be alone with nature: a number of smaller camps which do not have shops and restaurants, but do provide serviced and fully furnished air-conditioned accommodation to ensure a very comfortable stay. Private camps accommodate fewer than 20 people and visitors must book the entire camp. Bushveld camps can be booked on the normal basis for any number of guests. They are in great demand and even though one has to book up to 13 months in advance, they are generally oversubscribed. Equally popular are wilderness trails which enable groups of eight people to spend two days and three nights on safari in the company of an experienced game ranger.

THE SOUTHERN AREA

Jock of the Bushveld Private Camp

Wagon wheel gates, antique porcelain, rifles and other artifacts from the days of the transport riders reveal the theme of the Jock of the Bushveld camp. The camp was sponsored and planned by Cecily Mackie-Niven, daughter of Sir Percy FitzPatrick, and has a private waterhole and six huts which accommodate groups of 12 people. Its spotlessly maintained white thatched huts are

shaded by huge jackalberry trees and offer magnificent views over the Mntomene River below.

Malelane Private Camp

This camp dates back to 1925, when it was built as a culling post in order to control lion which were troubling local farmers. It has been tastefully refurbished and has five huts which accommodate 12 people. Malelane is situated on the banks of the Crocodile River, and game in the area includes lion, buffalo, cheetah, rhino, kudu and zebra.

Biyamiti Bushveld Camp

The most recently constructed of the bushveld camps, Biyamiti was built in May 1991 on a tree-lined river bank overlooking a waterhole in the vicinity of Crocodile Bridge. It has ten 5-bed and five 4-bed huts. The area is frequented by large buffalo, rhino, lion, elephant, wildebeest and zebra. It is the most easily accessible of the bushveld camps and is ideal if you wish to spend just a day or two in the park. Day walks are conducted from this camp.

THE CENTRAL AREA

Boulders Private Camp

Boulders – a quiet and quaint little place far from tourist routes – is situated south-west of Mopani camp at the foot of magnificent granite domes among which grow baobab and seringa trees. Twelve guests can be accommodated in superbly designed huts built on stilts (there are no fences) so as to blend in with the rustic surroundings.

Nwanetsi Private Camp

Nwanetsi lies in the foothills of the Lebombo Mountains near the Mozambique border. The Nwanetsi River (the name means 'reflections of the moon') is an attractive lily-covered stretch of water, and the camp which is built on its banks can accommodate 16 people. It is managed from Satara, which is the nearest supplier of petrol and food. Wildlife is plentiful in the area.

Roodewal Private Camp

Roodewal is situated on the banks of the Timbavati River, one of the most scenic stretches of water in the park. An attraction of the camp is a look-out platform built in a large nyala tree. Roodewal is situated on the border between the eastern grassland plains and the densely vegetated areas to the west. The camp can accommodate a maximum of 19 people.

Shimuwini Bushveld Camp

Shimuwini is set in an isolated area north-west of Letaba camp and its nine 5-bed huts and five 4-bed huts have commanding views over the Shimuwini Dam. There is a wide variety of game in the area, including buffalo, elephant, wild dog, rhino and nyala. Day walks are conducted from this camp.

Talamati Bushveld Camp

Situated near the dam close to Orpen gate, Talamati has ten 6-bed and five 4-bed huts overlooking the Nwaswitsontso River. The name appears to be something of a misnomer; it means 'lots of water' in Tsonga, but the river is almost always dry. There is, however, plentiful underground water and the clayey soil retains moisture for long periods of time; the consequent vegetation attracts large numbers of antelope and attendant predators. This is a prime area for sable antelope and lion.

THE NORTHERN AREA

Bateleur

Established in 1989, Bateleur is the smallest and oldest of the bushveld camps. It is a favourite with many who have stayed there, bird-watchers in particular. Its three 6-bed and four 4-bed huts have thatched roofs and whitewashed walls and are carefully arranged in a grove of well-established trees on the banks of the Mashokwe River. A viewing platform has been constructed overlooking a permanent waterhole built of concrete on the bank of the river and is often used as a mud bath by elephant. Like the river, it tends to dry up in the middle of winter. Animals to be seen around Bateleur include eland, nyala, elephant and tsessebe. Residents have exclusive access to two dams, namely Rooibosrand (where there are regular sightings of eland and sable) and Silverfish, which is an outstanding spot for seeing water birds.

Sirheni Bushveld Camp

On the banks of the Sirheni Dam one comes across what is reputed to be the finest bushveld camp in the park. It offers excellent game-viewing and bird-watching opportunities and is situated close to the scenic Mphongolo loop. If you are lucky you may see Lichtenstein's hartebeest, which were reintroduced to this area from Malawi. The camp has ten 6-bed and five 4-bed huts. Two hides have been built overlooking the river.

WILDERNESS TRAILS

There are seven wilderness trail camps in the park to accommodate groups of up to 8 people who take 3-day guided walks in the park, returning to camp each evening. There are no facilities for day visitors.

Boesman Wilderness Trail

This trail camp is situated in the heart of an area of immense archaeological importance. Stone Age tools, Iron Age smelting furnaces and San paintings are found here. The area contains most of the 100 paintings by these early hunter-gatherers found in the park, which record many of their hunting and wildlife experiences. The camp is situated only 7 kilometres from the Wolhuter Wilderness Trail base camp and hence the two trails meander through the same rocky hills densely vegetated with terminalia, sicklebush and red bush-willow. Kudu, impala, steenbok and rhino are commonly seen.

Metsi-Metsi Wilderness Trail

Considerable diversity of vegetation ensures that no two days at Metsi-Metsi will be alike. One day you can be walking in rocky gorges, the next on undulating plains, and the next in the steep foothills of the Lebombo Mountains. As a result, a wide variety of game can be found, including both black and white rhino, cheetah and leopard. The camp is situated behind Nwamuriwa Hill north-east of Tshokwane and has the thatched A-frame huts that are characteristic of the trail camps in Kruger.

Napi Wilderness Trail

Napi is situated at the confluence of the Biyamiti and Napi rivers and is the Kruger National Park's newest wilderness trail. Wooden A-frame huts are constructed high above the river, giving trailists outstanding views of the riverine wildlife. Sightings of white rhino are virtually guaranteed and you can also expect to encounter buffalo, elephant and lion. As is the case with other trails, you should not expect to walk more than 15 kilometres in a day.

Wolhuter Wilderness Trail

This was the first wilderness trail to be established (in 1979) and was named after Harry Wolhuter, who became a legend after he defended himself against a lion using only a small sheath knife. The camp is fenced and alive with birds, animals and insects. Set in an unspoilt wilderness dominated by granite outcrops, it is a restful place with its own waterhole. The outcrops are inhabited by many white rhino – one group of trailists spotted 57 of these animals in three days!

Sweni Wilderness Trail

Widely regarded as the most scenic of all the wilderness trails, Sweni is also one of the least rigorous, being situated in the flat central plains of the Kruger National Park. These verdant grasslands attract large herds of buffalo, elephant, kudu, wildebeest and giraffe and because of the density of antelope there are many lion (with prides of up to 40 individuals), hyaena and jackal in the area. White rhino are frequently encountered on the trail, and the occasional black rhino as well. The A-frame thatched huts are perched on stilts on the edge of the Sweni River amid clumps of ilala palms.

Nyalaland Trail

During one summer a group of ornithologists identified 186 birds on the Nyalaland Trail! Although this is exceptional, birdwatching is astoundingly good in this area, which is reputed to be one of the leading botanical areas in the world. Mottled spinetails nest in a baobab in the camp, situated in a grove of nyala trees. Walks through the area take trailists through riverine and baobab forests and underneath huge sycamore and Natal mahogany trees. A highlight of the trail is a visit to one of the only San paintings in the park to depict elephants.

OPPOSITE: *Bateleur, one of the Kruger Park's smallest bushveld camps, offers secluded accommodation close to the Mashokwe River.*
BELOW: *Walkers on the Wolhuter Wilderness Trail take a rest and enjoy the unforgettable spectacle of an elephant passing by.*
BOTTOM: *Lovely Shimuwini – meaning 'the place of the baobab tree' – takes its name from a nearby baobab that has a circumference of some 17 metres.*

KRUGER PARK ADVISORY

WHEN TO GO

Many visitors to the park are unsure of the best time to visit, but both seasons offer markedly different wilderness experiences. The dry winter (April to September) is best if you wish to see large numbers of game. As many rivers and waterholes dry up, animals frequent artificial water supplies and perennial rivers which are usually close to game-viewing roads. Trees lose their leaves and vegetation is generally less dense. Temperatures are milder, averaging about 23 °C, while nights may be cool (6 °C).

Summer (October to March) has a charm all of its own. The summer thunderstorms start in early November in Mpumalanga, and the dry, leafless trees adopt their summer foliage, flowers blossom in the veld, and antelope begin to drop their young.

The afternoon thunderstorms provide welcome relief from the heat of the day (30 °C to over 40 °C). The southern areas of the park are the coolest because of their higher altitude and rainfall. Pretoriuskop experiences the most precipitation (up to 800 millimetres), while the northern areas are the driest (up to 500 millimetres).

Summer is an excellent time for bird-watchers, as migratory species from as far away as Siberia flock to the area to breed.

WHAT TO TAKE

Sunscreen, mosquito repellent and net, hat, swimming costume, photographic equipment (including a beanbag), binoculars and sunglasses. Consult a pharmacist or doctor for appropriate anti-malaria tablets as malaria is still a problem (start the course three weeks before entering the area). In summer and winter light garments will suffice, but take warm clothing for winter evenings.

RESERVATIONS & INFORMATION

Applications for accommodation may be submitted up to 13 months in advance to the Chief Director, Reservations, National Parks Board, PO Box 787, Pretoria 0001, or by telephoning Pretoria (012) 343-1991, Cape Town (021) 22-2810 or Skukuza (013) 735-5159. The SA National Parks have a website at www.parks-sa.co.za, where the Kruger Park has a homepage. In future it will be possible to make bookings through this page. School holidays are very popular for visits – at such times, stays in the park may not exceed 7 days. Wilderness Trails are closed in December and January.

REGULATIONS

The speed limit is 50 kilometres on tarred roads and 40 kilometres per hour on other roads (there are speed traps, so be careful to stick to the limits). Within camps, the speed limit is 10 kilometres per hour.

You may not drive on unmarked roads and you must stay in your vehicle at all times, unless you are at an approved get-out point. Pets are not allowed and firearms must be declared at the entrance gates. Feeding of the animals and birds is strictly prohibited.

GETTING ABOUT

Cars may be hired at Skukuza. A vehicle in which you are high off the road is best, as your view will be better. Visitors to the park often ask whether they should drive along tar or dirt roads; game-viewing is better along tar roads, since animals avoid the dusty leaves next to dirt roads.

WILDLIFE

The largest concentrations of game occur in the central and southern areas towards the eastern half of the park. Game that may be seen includes elephant, giraffe, buffalo, lion, cheetah, rhino, leopard, kudu and impala. The northern areas are elephant and buffalo country. More than 500 bird species inhabit the park, with the best viewing in camps, at picnic areas and in river valleys. The visitors' book in each camp is an ideal way to find out up-to-date information about sightings.

GUIDED DRIVES

Guided day or half-day drives in an open vehicle are offered at Skukuza, Letaba and Berg en Dal. Bookings can be made at the reception desks. Night drives, conducted in open vehicles from all rest camps, bushveld camps and Phalaborwa Gate, start half an hour

before gate closing time and provide a great opportunity to observe the nocturnal animals such as leopard, civet, porcupine, bushbaby and all the owls and other night birds. Book in advance through the reservations offices.

GATES

January: gates open at 05h00 and close at 18h30 (entry gates open at 05h30).
February – March: all gates open at 05h30 and close at 18h00.
April: all gates open at 06h00 and close at 17h30.
May – August: all gates open at 06h30 and close at 17h30.
September: all gates open at 06h00 and close at 18h00.
October: all gates open at 05h30 and close at 18h00.
November – December: gates open at 04h30 and close at 18h30 (entry gates to the park open at 05h30).

CAMP RECEPTIONS AND SHOPS

These open at 08h00 and close half an hour after gates close.

RESTAURANTS

Breakfast: 07h00 to 09h00. Lunch: 12h00 to 14h00. Dinner: 18h00 to 21h00.

ACCOMMODATION

This may be occupied from 12h00 on your day of arrival and must be vacated before 09h00 on the day of your departure.

REST CAMPS

Berg en Dal is a large camp in a mountain setting with cottages, huts, lodges and an outstanding camping and caravan site.

There is an in-camp trail, swimming pool, environmental and educational centre, petrol station, shop, restaurant and laundry. Facilities are available for day visitors.
Crocodile Bridge, a small camp overlooking the Crocodile River, has camping and caravan sites, self-catering huts, a petrol station, shop and laundry.
Letaba, one of the park's larger camps, has guest cottages, huts, camping and caravan sites, facilities for day visitors, a trail, environmental and information centres, elephant museum, vehicle emergency service, shop, restaurant and laundry.
Lower Sabie, set in the foothills of the Lebombo Mountains overlooking the Sabie River, has guest cottages, huts, a petrol station, shop, restaurant and laundry.
Mopani has a swimming pool, comfortable huts, facilities for day visitors and conferences. There is a trail, petrol station, shop, restaurant, bar for residents and laundry.
Olifants offers superb views and has facilities for day visitors. It has guest cottages, huts, an educational display, petrol station, shop, restaurant and laundry.
Orpen is a small camp with self-catering huts and has a satellite camping site nearby at Maroela. Day visitors are permitted and there is a petrol station and shop.
Pretoriuskop, one of the larger camps, is situated in a mountainous region of the national park. There is a swimming pool, facilities for day visitors, camping and caravan sites, guest cottages, huts, a restaurant, a petrol station, a shop and a laundry.
Punda Maria is a charming 'old world' camp which has family cottages, huts, camping sites, facilities for day visitors, an in-camp trail, a petrol station, shop, restaurant and laundry
Satara is in the game-rich central section of the park and has a car wash, vehicle emergency service, petrol station, educational display, shop, restaurant, facilities for day visitors, camping and caravan sites, guest cottages, huts and a laundry.
Shingwedzi is in elephant country, and has a swimming pool, restaurant, shop, laundromat, petrol station, camping and caravan site, facilities for day visitors, huts and an educational display.
Skukuza, the largest camp in the park, has museums, cottages, huts, educational and environmental centres, restaurants, shops, facilities for day visitors, camping and caravan sites, a petrol station, vehicle emergency service, car hire, airport, post office, bank, a doctor and laundromat.

PRIVATE CAMPS

There are eight private camps, each of which accommodates fewer than 20 people and must be booked *en bloc*. The huts have all facilities for a comfortable stay and are furnished. Guests are required to bring their own provisions, which are cooked for them by the staff. There are no facilities for day visitors. See p 44 for more details.

BUSHVELD CAMPS

There are six small self-catering camps in remote areas of the park which need not be booked in their entirety. There are no facilities for day visitors. See p 44 for details.
Camping Only
The camps at Maroela and Balule are for camping and caravanning only (no facilities for day visitors). A tented camp has been erected at Tamboti, close to Orpen Gate, which has safari-style tents.

PHONES

Public telephones are available at all rest camps and bushveld camps, with cellphone reception at most larger rest camps.

FURTHER READING

A map of the park is available at rest camps. *Getaway* magazine featured the Kruger rest camps between October 1994 and January 1997. The following are also very informative reading:
Bannister, A. and Ryan, B., *National Parks of South Africa*, Struik, Cape Town, 1993.
Braack, Leo, *Kruger National Park – A Visitor's Guide*, Struik, Cape Town, 1992.
De Graaff, G., *Animals of the Kruger National Park*, Struik, Cape Town, 1992.
Fourie, P.F., *Kruger National Park , Questions & Answers*, Struik, Cape Town, 1992.
Kruger National Park, *Make the Most of Kruger*, Jacana, Johannesburg, 1993.
Paynter, David and Nussey, Wilf, *Kruger – Portrait of a National Park*, Southern Book Publishers, Johannesburg, 1992.
Sinclair, Ian and Whyte, Ian, *Field Guide to the Birds of the Kruger National Park*, Struik, Cape Town, 1991.

OPPOSITE ABOVE: *Shingwedzi, the largest of the northerly camps, is set in riverine forest frequented by a number of the park's leopards.*
OPPOSITE BELOW: *Visitors are treated to a close-up view of the park's largest resident.*
LEFT: *The swimming pool at Mopani Rest Camp – one of its most popular facilities during the warmer summer months.*

INDEX

Main entries are listed in bold;
photographs are listed in italics.

Struik Publishers (Pty) Ltd
*(a member of The Struik Publishing
Group (Pty) Ltd)
Cornelis Struik House, 80 McKenzie Street
Cape Town 8001*

Reg. No.: 54/00965/07

*First published in 1994
Second impression 1996
Third impression 1998*

*Text © David Rogers
Map © Loretta Chegwidden
Photographs © individual photo-
graphers and/or their agents as follows:*

K S Begg: *pp. 21 (top), 30 (bottom).*
Gerald Cubitt: *p. 10 (top), front cover.*
Nigel Dennis: *pp. 1, 2, 3, 6, 7, 8, 9, 11
(top and bottom), 12, 13 (top and bottom), 15, 16 (top and bottom), 17 (top),
18, 19, 20 (top and bottom), 21 (bottom),
22, 23 (top, centre left and right, bottom),
25 (top and bottom left), 26, 27, 28 (top),
32 (top, bottom left and right), 33, 34, 35,
37 (top and bottom right), 39 (top, centre
and bottom), 40, 41, 42, 43 (top, bottom
left and right), 44 and back cover.* **James
Stevenson-Hamilton Collection:** *p. 9
(top).* **Lorna Stanton:** *pp. 17 (bottom),
24, 29, 30 (top left and right), 31, 36, 38
(left and right), 45 (top and bottom), 46
(top and bottom), 47.* © **Struik Image
Library: Photographer Peter
Pickford:** *pp. 10 (bottom), 14, 25 (bottom
right), 37 (bottom left).* **David Steele:**
p. 28 [Photo Access].

*Project Co-ordinator: Marje Hemp
Copy Editor: Jan Schaafsma
Editorial Assistant: Christine Didcott
Designer: René Greeff
Design Assistant: Lyndall Hamilton
Typeset by Suzanne Fortescue, Struik
DTP, Cape Town
Reproduction by Hirt & Carter
Cape (Pty) Ltd
Printed and bound by Kyodo Printing
Co (Pte) Ltd, Singapore*

*All rights reserved. No part of this publi-
cation may be reproduced, stored in a
retrieval system or transmitted in any
form or by any means, electronic,
mechanical, photocopying, recording or
otherwise, without the prior written per-
mission of the copyright owners.*

ISBN 1 86825 608 1

Acknowledgements
*The publishers and author wish to
thank the National Parks Board for their
kind assistance, Nigel Dennis for his
invaluable contribution to the photography and text, and Ian Milne,
Information Officer at Skukuza, for
ensuring that the information in this
guide is factual and up to date.*